D1307992

MOUNTAIN GORILLAS
IN DANGER

BY RITA RITCHIE • PHOTOGRAPHY BY MICHAEL NICHOLS

Gareth Stevens Children's Books
MILWAUKEE

A note from the publisher: Today, the existence of the mountain gorilla is limited to one region on earth — the rain forests of central Africa's Virunga volcanoes. Through conservation efforts and educational programs, the mountain gorilla has a chance for continued survival. We hope that books like this one will help young readers appreciate the value of a species and its natural right to live alongside humankind.

For a free color catalog describing Gareth Stevens' list of high-quality children's books, call 1-800-341-3569 (USA) or 1-800-461-9120 (Canada).

Library of Congress Cataloging-in-Publication Data

Ritchie, Rita
 Mountain gorillas in danger / by Rita Ritchie ; photographs by Michael Nichols.
   p. cm. -- (Animal world)
 Includes bibliographical references and index.
 Summary: Discusses mountain gorillas in the rain forests of the Virunga Mountains of central Africa, an endangered species due to poachers, farmers, and collectors.
 ISBN 0-8368-0447-3
 1. Gorilla--Juvenile literature. 2. Gorilla--Virunga--Juvenile literature. 3. Endangered species--Virunga--Juvenile literature. 4. Wildlife conservation--Virunga--Juvenile literature. [1. Gorilla. 2. Zoology—Virunga.] I. Nichols, Michael, ill. II. Title. II. Series: Animal world (Milwaukee, Wis.)
 QL737.P96R58   1991   91-10801

A Gareth Stevens Children's Book edition

Edited, designed, and produced by
Gareth Stevens Children's Books
1555 North RiverCenter Drive, Suite 201
Milwaukee, Wisconsin 53212, USA

Mountain Gorillas in Danger is based on the book *Gorillas*, by Michael Nichols and George Schaller, originally published by Aperture Foundation, Inc. Aperture publishes a periodical, books, and portfolios of fine photography to communicate with serious photographers and creative people everywhere. A complete catalog is available upon request. Address: Aperture, 20 East 23 Street, New York, NY 10010.

Series editor: Rita Reitci
Series and cover design: Laurie Shock
Consulting editor: Virginia Harrison

Printed in the United States of America

1 2 3 4 5 6 7 8 9 97 96 95 94 93 92 91

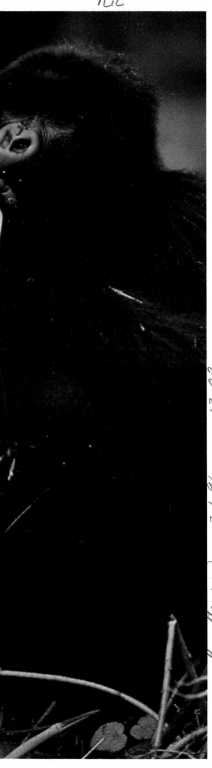

CONTENTS

Home in the Mountains 4
Quiet Gorillas 6
Gorillas in Danger 8
Danger in Nature 10
Danger from Farmers 12
Danger from Poachers 14
Danger from New Leaders 16
How People Can Help 18
Patrolling the Virungas 20
Farmers Helping 22
Jobs for People...............................24
Studying Gorillas 26
More Gorillas..................................28

Gorilla Facts 30
More Books to Read 30
Places to Write 31
Glossary 31
Index 32

Words in **bold type** are explained in the glossary.

Home in the Mountains

Mountain gorillas live among the Virunga Mountains. These are six inactive volcanoes in central Africa. Their steep slopes are covered with **rain forests**. Most days there are cool and damp, and it often rains.

Mountain gorillas eat and sleep in the thick tangle of trees, plants, vines, and mosses. There are only about 400 mountain gorillas still alive. If people do not help, these unusual animals may die out forever.

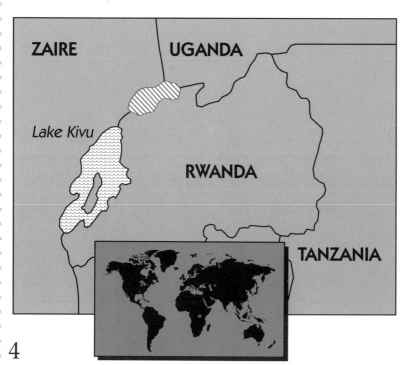

ZAIRE UGANDA

Lake Kivu

RWANDA

TANZANIA

◀ Parts of Zaire, Rwanda, and Uganda (red on small map below) border the Virunga volcano range, which is home to mountain gorillas (green on large map).

▲ The heather plant grows to a giant size in the mountain gorillas' rain forest home.

▲ Inset: This lake fills the crater of one of the inactive Virunga volcanoes. The streaks were made by the movement of stars during the long time it took to make this photograph.

HAND SIZE, FOOT SIZE
A **silverback's** hand can be six inches (15.2 cm) wide. A human male's hand is only about half that size. A silverback's foot can be 12 inches (30.5 cm) long and is much wider than a human male's foot.

◄ Despite their fierce appearance, these gorillas just want to live their lives in peace. Gorillas become threatening only when protecting themselves or their families.

Wild celery grows to eight feet (2.4 m) tall. It tastes bitter, but gorillas enjoy eating it after they peel it. ▶

Quiet Gorillas

Mountain gorillas have **adapted** to living in their high, cool mountains. They have thicker hair, shorter arms and legs, and a bigger chest than low-land gorillas.

Gorillas, monkeys, and humans all belong to the **primate** group. Gorillas roam in family groups, eating leaves, the insides of tree branches, bamboo, wild celery, nettles, thistles, and other kinds of plants.

The mountain gorillas have strong teeth and powerful arms. They can fight but would rather live in peace.

Gorillas in Danger

Mountain gorillas face dangers from nature, humans, and other gorillas. Because mountain gorillas must grow for years before they can become parents, the group will die out if too many adult gorillas die.

A female is eight years old before she can **mate** and have a baby. A male is about 12 years old before he can mate. At this age, he becomes a silverback, with white hair on his back.

The gorilla infant remains close to his mother during the first few years of life. He's always within an arm's reach. ▼

▲ Silverbacks are twice as big as female adult gorillas. These males weigh about 375 pounds (170 kg). Females weigh about 200 pounds (90 kg).

This youngster is not old
enough yet to help defend
the family from harm. ▶

Danger in Nature

Gorilla family groups grow very slowly, but they can be destroyed very quickly. A gorilla baby grows inside its mother for nine months before being born. The female will not have another baby for three or four years. But if her **infant** dies, she will have another baby much sooner.

About half the infants die before they are a year old. They have accidents or get diseases and worms that make them weak. Even adults can get sick.

GORILLA GROWTH
Female gorillas are usually pregnant or nursing their young. Females cannot become pregnant while their infants are nursing. And since infants nurse for about three years, the gorilla family group grows very slowly.

◀ Soon this baby will be strong enough to ride on its mother's back.

The mother of this baby is always watching to see that it doesn't hurt itself. ▼

◀ Farmland seen through the trees. Much of the mountain gorillas' forest has been cleared of trees so people can grow crops.

Danger from Farmers

People have turned much of the mountain forests into farms, so there is less land and less food for the gorillas. When mountain gorillas eat the farm crops, the farmers try to kill them.

Some people **graze** their cattle in the gorilla forests. The cattle eat the gorillas' food, dirty their land, and tear up the earth with their hooves. Cattle ruin the land for gorillas.

A boy of the Hutu tribe cares for his cattle. The Hutu tribe — one of three main tribes in Rwanda — uses the rain forest to graze livestock. ▼

Danger from Poachers

Hunting is not allowed in the
Virunga gorilla forests. But some
hunters, called **poachers**, kill adult
gorillas so they can sell their infants
to a zoo or to a collector. These
gorilla infants usually die later.

Poachers also set traps for other animals, such as buffalo and antelope.
Gorillas get caught in these traps.
Trying to break free, they may lose a
hand or a foot. Later, if their wounds
get **infected**, they might die.

The injured hand of a
female gorilla. She
caught it in a snare
when she was young. ▼

▲ This silverback's fingers were cut off by a poacher's snare. He survived, but many injured gorillas die when their wounds become infected.

A wire snare. Poachers hide traps in the grasses of the forest to trap antelope or buffalo. Gorillas are often caught instead. ▶

Danger from New Leaders

The silverback is the leader of his family. He keeps order and protects his family from enemies. If he is killed, another silverback may take over the family.

When gorillas are left alone, the new leader will care for the family. But if they are threatened, the new silverback may kill all the infants. This makes the females mate with him right away and bear his babies. Danger makes the silverback want his own babies quickly.

▲ A silverback and a juvenile gorilla. In raising their young, adult gorillas normally strengthen family ties. But when faced with constant danger, an adult male gorilla may try to kill the infants. Then the females will mate with him, and he can have babies of his own.

A new silverback leader. The silverback must be a strong leader so he can look after his group. ▶

How People Can Help

One way to help mountain gorillas is to tell people about them. Many villagers living in the Virungas have never seen a gorilla. But photographers have made movies of these animals. They show these movies in the villages. Now the people can learn that gorillas need to be protected.

Teachers take children into the mountains to see the gorillas. Then the children's parents become interested in helping save the gorillas, too.

Thousands of villagers come to see movies about their gorilla neighbors. When they learn about them, they want to help save them. ▼

▲ Villagers in Zaire are beginning to respect the gorilla. The animal is becoming a national symbol.

A Hutu boy with a drawing of tourists photographing the gorillas. He has seen the gentle beasts himself. ▶

19

▲ This man is one of many hired to patrol the parks where the gorillas live. He watches for poachers and their traps.

◀ This antelope is already dead, but when the guards find a live trapped animal, they turn it loose.

Patrolling the Virungas

Many guards now **patrol** the Virunga gorilla forests. They look for traps and **snares** set by poachers. They pull these apart and set free any animals that may be caught in them. Sadly, many of these animals die before they are found. The guards arrest the poachers they catch and send them to jail.

The guards also drive out the cattle that graze in the forest. They make the cattle herders pay a big **fine**.

This is a buffalo snare that poachers bury in mudholes. They connect their snares to logs, which catch in the trees and keep the trapped buffalo from moving on. ▶

Farmers Helping

Farmers in the Virungas need more land. They want to clear away the forests and grow crops. But without the forests, the crops would soon fail.

The roots of the forest plants hold the soil in place. Rain soaks into the soil and runs into many streams that water the farms farther away. Even in the dry periods, there is water for crops and people. To keep getting enough water, farmers must help save the gorilla forests.

These trees on the Virunga slopes keep the soil in place. The soil stores the water needed by the wild plants and the crops that feed gorillas and farmers alike.

▲ Potatoes are a main
crop of the Hutu tribe.
These potatoes grow
where gorillas once
foraged.

▲ Visiting groups are kept small to keep from alarming the gorillas.

◄ Tourists travel a long way into the gorilla forest. They must take their food supply with them. Hired porters often help carry the load.

Jobs for People

Working to save the gorillas provides jobs and money for the local people. Many people earn money selling supplies or working in the gorilla forests.

Guards keep cattle and poachers away from the gorillas. Trackers find snares and traps. Porters carry loads and do other camp work. Guides take small groups of tourists into the forests to see the gorillas. But tourists can be a danger, too, because they can pass on diseases to the gorillas.

These visitors traveled thousands of miles just to see the gorillas. ▶

Studying Gorillas

Many scientists now study the mountain gorillas and how they fit into their **habitat**. Experts are also learning more about the plants and other animals of the rain forest that surrounds the gorillas. Some of their discoveries may help humans.

Because gorillas and humans are primates, knowing about gorillas can help us understand more about people. We may find out how humans form into different kinds of groups. We can learn about how people act in these groups.

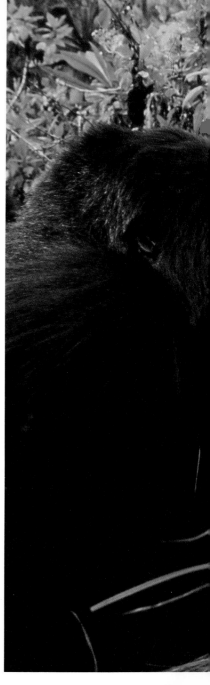

◀ Through long, complete studies, scientists have discovered that gorillas have a mothering and caring family bond, very much like a human family.

▲ A human researcher
studies a gorilla, which
seems to be studying
the human!

More Gorillas

The Virunga gorilla forests lie in three connecting parks. These parks are in the countries of Rwanda, Zaire, and Uganda. Nearly all of Uganda's mountain gorillas live in the Impenetrable Forest nearby. In these four parks, the mountain gorillas and their habitat are protected.

Many people still want to use the gorilla forests for farming, logging, hunting, and grazing cattle. Others see the need to protect the gorillas' home. Because of their efforts, the number of mountain gorillas is slowly getting larger.

Background: Giant lobelia plants stand 10 feet (3 m) tall. Gorillas use their leafy tops for nesting material and food.

Inset: Scientists have opened the world's eyes to the needs of mountain gorillas. Their future depends on us.

MOUNTAIN GORILLAS IN DANGER

Gorilla Facts

The Virunga mountain range where mountain gorillas live in Africa is an area only 40 miles (60 km) long and 6 to 12 miles (9-19 km) wide. The Impenetrable Forest, the other home of mountain gorillas, is even smaller.

Gorillas walk on all fours. They clench their hands into fists as they go along. This is called knuckle-walking. A mother with a new infant carries it cradled in one arm, using the other for knuckle-walking. When a gorilla feels threatened, it will rear on its hind legs. Full-grown male gorillas can stand six feet (1.8 m) tall!

Gorillas are among our closest living relatives. These animals have many things in common with humans. In fact, gorillas and humans are so much alike that gorillas can catch colds from humans! Only chimpanzees are more closely related to humans.

More Books to Read

Listed here are more books about gorillas. If you would like to read them, look in your library or ask an adult to order them for you at a bookstore.

Endangered Animals. Stone (Childrens Press)
Gargantua: The Mighty Gorilla.
      Glendinning and Glendinning (Garrard)
Gorilla. McClung (Morrow Junior Books)
Gorilla, Gorilla. Fenner (Random)
How Mountain Gorillas Live. Harrison (Gareth Stevens)
Monkeys and Apes. Barrett (Watts)
Monkeys, Apes, and Other Primates. Bogard (Young
      Discovery Library)
Mountain Gorillas and Their Young.
      Harrison (Gareth Stevens)
Patti's Pet Gorilla. Mauser (Macmillan)
Tropical Rainforests Around the World. Landau (Watts)
Which Way to the Nearest Wilderness? Springstubb (Dell)
Wildlife Alert. Stuart (National Geographic)

Places To Write

If you would like to find out more about the problems facing mountain gorillas and other rare animals around the world, write to the groups listed below. When you write, be sure to say exactly what you want to know. Always include your full name, address, and age, and enclose a stamped envelope addressed to yourself.

Environment Canada
Canadian Wildlife Service
   Publications
17th Floor, PVM 351
St. Joseph Boulevard
Hull, Quebec K1A 0H3

Rainforest Action Network
301 Broadway, Suite A
San Francisco, California
   94133

World Wildlife Fund
   (Canada)
90 Eglindon Avenue E,
   Suite 504
Toronto, Ontario M4P 2Z7

World Wildlife Fund (U.S.)
1250 24th Street, NW
Washington, DC 20037

Glossary

Adapt: To change over a period of time to fit in better with the surroundings. For example, mountain gorillas have adapted to their cool environment by growing thicker fur than lowland gorillas.

Fine: Money paid in place of going to jail. Fines are often punishment for less serious crimes. For example, anyone caught grazing cattle in gorilla areas is fined, but anyone caught hurting or killing gorillas is jailed for five years.

Graze: To feed on grass or similar plants. People used to let their cows graze in gorilla feeding areas, robbing the gorillas of their food. Now this is against the law.

Habitat: Where an animal or a plant belongs; its natural home. The habitat of mountain gorillas is a very small mountain area covered by rain forest. If these homes are destroyed or changed too much, the gorillas will no longer be able to live there.

Infant: A baby. Baby gorillas are infants for about three years. During this time, they stay close to their mothers, who feed and protect them.

Infected: Diseased from germs. Any wound that is not kept clean can get infected. If a gorilla's wound is not treated, an infection can spread until it kills the gorilla, even if it survived the initial wound.

Mate: To pair a male and female to have babies.

Patrol: To move about an area looking for signs of trouble. Guards patrol gorilla areas to protect mountain gorillas. They look for signs of hunters or snares, or anything else that could hurt the gorillas.

Poacher: A hunter who kills animals that are protected by law. They then sell parts of these animals for high prices. These criminals have killed so many gorillas, elephants, rhinoceroses, and other rare animals that soon there may be none left. We can stop poachers by refusing to buy any of the things made from rare animals and by catching and jailing these hunters.

Primate: A member of the animal group that includes humans, gorillas, and monkeys. Primates are the most intelligent of all animals. They easily adjust to changes and new things around them.

Rain forest: A thick forest, or jungle, where it rains at least 70 to 100 inches (180-250 cm) a year. Most rain forests have wet and dry seasons. These forests generally grow in the tropics, either in lowlands or on mountain slopes.

Silverback: A full-grown male gorilla over twelve years old. Each gorilla family group has at least one silverback. The silverback is the group's leader. He protects the group from outsiders.

Snare: A trap set to catch an animal. Usually a snare is a wire loop that tightens around the arm or leg of an animal that is caught in it. Many gorillas are hurt or killed by snares set by poachers hunting for other animals.

Index

Africa 4-5

family groups 7, 11, 16, 26
farmers and farming (in
    the gorillas' habitat)
    12-13, 22-23, 28
feeding 7, 13, 23
females 8, 11

gorillas' likeness to
    humans 7, 26

habitat 4, 26
Hutu tribe 13, 19, 23

Impenetrable Forest 28
infants 8, 11, 14, 16

males 7, 8, 15, 16-17
mating 8, 11, 16

nursing 11

physical features of
    gorillas 7, 8
poachers 14-15, 20-21, 25
primates, other 7
    humans 7, 8, 26
    monkeys 7

rain forests 4, 26
Rwanda 4, 13, 28

silverbacks (see males)
snares 14, 15, 21, 25

Uganda 4, 28

Virunga volcanoes 4-5, 14,
    18, 21, 22-23, 28

youngsters 9, 11, 16

Zaire 4, 19, 28